D1254660

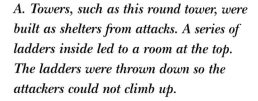

A. Towers, such as this round tower, were built as shelters from attacks. A series of ladders inside led to a room at the top. The ladders were thrown down so the attackers could not climb up.

B. This Celtic cross lies on a gravesite.

C. The ruins of a medieval castle that protected the monks living at Clonmacnoise monastery.

D. St. Kevin started this monastery in Southern Ireland around 550 A.D. The church was built around 1050 A.D.

E. Some of Ireland's ancient kings were buried in the monastery's cemetery at Clonmacnoise

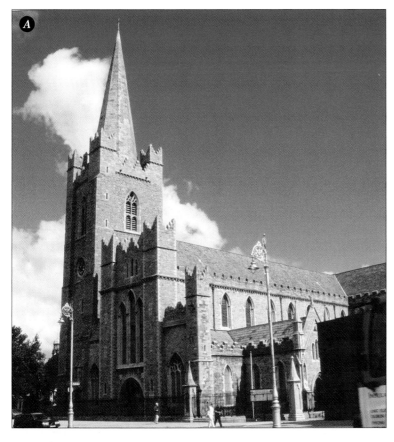

A. St. Patrick's Cathedral is Ireland's largest church. It stands near a stream where St. Patrick baptized Christians in 420 A.D.

B. Jonathan Swift wrote Gulliver's Travels. He was also the head, or dean, of St. Patrick's Cathedral in 1713.

C. The interior of St. Patrick's is decorated with monuments, brass and sculptures. This is where the choir sits. The altar is at the back.

D. The tomb of Archbishop Saunford who died in 1271 is in St. Patrick's Cathedral.

The Irish love sports

A. Kerry fans come in all ages. Here dad, son, and granddad make their way to the football stadium.   .

B. Nothing could keep these football (soccer) fans from watching Ireland compete in an important game to qualify for the World Cup.

C. The whole family gets together to cheer on County Kerry against County Tipperary.

IRELAND
the culture

Erinn Banting

A Bobbie Kalman Book

The Lands, Peoples, and Cultures Series

Crabtree Publishing Company

www.crabtreebooks.com

The Lands, Peoples, and Cultures Series

Created by Bobbie Kalman

Coordinating editor
Ellen Rodger

Project editor
P.A. Finlay

Production coordinator
Rosie Gowsell

Project development, photo research, and design
First Folio Resource Group, Inc.
Erinn Banting
Tom Dart
Greg Duhaney
Söğüt Y. Güleç
Debbie Smith

Editing
Carolyn Black

Prepress and printing
Worzalla Publishing Company

Consultants
Brian Costello; Dissolving Boundaries Through Technology in Education; Stephen Guidon; Matthew Keenan; Darren Kenny; Sean MacMathuna; Michael J. McCann, InfoMarex; Liam Merwick; Jennifer O'Connell and North Dublin National School Project's 5th class; Michael O'Gorman; Paul Quinn; Chris Stephenson; Colin Stephenson

Special Thanks
Thanks to Ivoane Mcmorough who connected us with her wonderful friends in Ireland. Thanks to Patrick and Creena MacNeill who passed their love for Ireland to Crabtree Publishing. Thanks to Jack McCormack of St. Saviour's Amateur Boxing Club.

Photographs
Art Resource/Image Select: p. 27 (bottom); Art Resource/The Tate Gallery: p. 19 (bottom); Art Resource/Victoria and Albert Museum, London: p. 27 (top); Art Resource/Werner Forman Archive: p. 17 (both); The Bridgeman Art Library: p. 28 (left); The Bridgeman Art Library/The Frederick Gallery, Dublin, Ireland: p. 19 (top); The Bridgeman Art Library/Simon Marsden/The Marsden Archive, UK: p. 6 (bottom); Corbis/Magma Photo News Inc./Tom Bean: p. 21; Corbis/Magma Photo News Inc./Lois Ellen: p. 12 (left); Corbis/Magma Photo News Inc./Melanie Grizzel: p. 16 (left); Corbis/Magma Photo News Inc./ Dallas and John Heaton: p. 16 (right); Corbis/Magma Photo News Inc./Jan-Butchofsky Houser: p. 20 (bottom); Corbis/Magma Photo News Inc./Hulton-Deutsch Collection: p. 28 (right); Corbis/Magma Photo News Inc./Robbie Jack: p. 29; Corbis/Magma Photo News Inc./Stephanie Maze: p. 24; Corbis/Magma Photo News Inc./David Muench: p. 3; Corbis/Magma Photo News Inc./Michael St. Maur Sheil: p. 9 (right), p. 15 (both); Corbis/Magma Photo News Inc./Geray Sweeney: p. 11 (bottom); Corbis/Magma Photo News Inc./David Turnley: p. 25 (right); Dan Good: p.16 inset; Marc Crabtree: cover, front endpages p. 1 (all), p. 2 (top left, bottom left, top right, middle right), p. 3 (top), rear endpages p. 1 (top left, middle left), p. 2, p. 5 (bottom), p. 7 (right), p. 9 (top), p. 20 (top), p. 22 (bottom), p. 25 (bottom); Peter Crabtree: title page, front endpages p. 2 (bottom right), p. 3 (middle, bottom left), rear endpages p. 1 (bottom left, top right, bottom right), p. 2 (all), p. 3 (all), p. 23 (both); Hulton/Getty: p. 8; Rafael Macia/Photo Researchers: p. 22 (left); Peter Matthews: p. 4, p. 5 (top), p. 7 (left), p. 10, p. 11 (top), p. 13, p. 14 (both), p. 18 (top); North Wind Pictures: p. 6 (top), p. 26; Kay Shaw: p. 18 (bottom); Tim Thompson: p. 12 (right)

Illustrations
Dianne Eastman: icon
Dorota Lagida: pp. 30–31
David Wysotski, Allure Illustrations: back cover

Cover: The Celtic high cross from the eighth century is a symbol of Christianity often seen throughout Ireland.

Title page: Belfast Castle, built in 1870, is now a heritage center owned by the City of Belfast.

Icon: The Celtic harp, one of the national symbols of the Republic of Ireland, appears at the head of each section.

Back cover: Irish hares can most often be seen at night chewing grasses and young trees with their large teeth.

Published by
Crabtree Publishing Company

PMB 16A,
350 Fifth Avenue
Suite 3308
New York
N.Y. 10118

612 Welland Avenue
St. Catharines
Ontario, Canada
L2M 5V6

73 Lime Walk
Headington
Oxford OX3 7AD
United Kingdom

Cataloging in Publication Data
Banting, Erinn
    Ireland the culture / Erinn Banting.
        p.cm.-- (The lands, peoples, and cultures series)
Includes index.
    ISBN 0-7787-9351-6 (RLB) -- ISBN 0-7787-9719-8 (pbk.)
    1. Ireland--Civilization--Juvenile literature. 2. Ireland--Social life and customs--Juvenile literature. [1. Ireland--Civilization.] I. Title. II. Series.
    DA925.B36 2002
    941.5--dc21
                                2001007749
                                LC

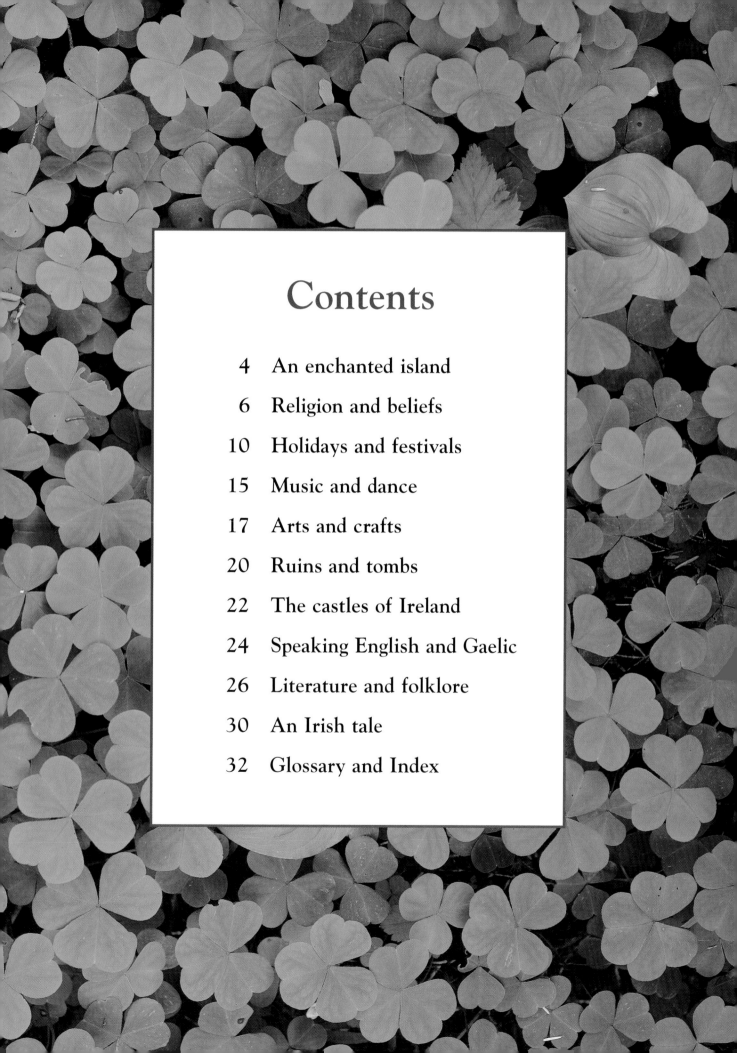

Contents

More than 2,000 years ago, the Celts, or Gaels as they called themselves, came to the island of Ireland from Europe. The **customs**, traditions, stories, and Gaelic language that they brought with them are still alive today.

There are many Celtic **myths** about how Ireland got its Gaelic name, Éire. One myth tells the story of a group of warriors, called the Tuatha de Dannan, who used magical powers to fight the Milesians, a people from Spain who wanted to take over Ireland. Banbha was the first warrior to cast a spell on the Milesians, but her magic did not work. Fodhla was no more successful.

Éirí tried something different. She sat on a hilltop and threw gigantic balls of mud at the enemies. When the balls of mud hit the bottom of the hill, they broke into thousands of warriors. The warriors fought bravely against the Milesians, but lost the battle. When the Milesians took over the land, they named it Éire, after Éirí, because they were so impressed by her magic.

(top) During a Saint Patrick's Day parade in Dublin, the capital of the Republic of Ireland, people with painted faces and brightly colored costumes pull a dragon float down the street.

A flutist plays a traditional folk song at the Feakle Traditional Music Weekend in county Clare. The Irish are known for their national and international music festivals.

A common ground

Since the Celts, many other groups, such as the Vikings, Normans, and English, have arrived on Ireland's shores. People in Ireland share a common history and common traditions, yet political and religious differences have separated them. Ireland is divided into Northern Ireland, which is part of the **United Kingdom**, and the Republic of Ireland, or Éire, which is an **independent** country. After decades of disagreement, people in both parts of Ireland are learning to accept each others' differences.

Blarney Castle, built in 1446, is home to the Blarney stone, which, when kissed, is said to give the "gift of the gab."

Religion and beliefs

For thousands of years, religion has influenced daily life in Ireland. It has united people in the south, but divided people in the north. Many Roman Catholics and Protestants in Northern Ireland live in different neighborhoods, shop at different stores, and go to different schools. Their religious differences have caused years of fighting. Today, violence in Northern Ireland is less frequent. People of other religions, such as Judaism and Islam, also practice their faiths in many parts of the land.

Druidism

The ancient Celts practiced a religion called Druidism. They believed that objects in nature had spirits which people should **worship** and honor, and that many gods and goddesses controlled the world. Druids were the leaders of the Celtic church. These priests and priestesses used their special powers to heal the sick and talk to spirits.

A Druid prepares for a religious ceremony by collecting mistletoe, a plant which Druids considered sacred.

A stone carving that is thousands of years old shows the heads of three Celtic gods. Celts worshiped heads because they believed heads were the center of the soul.

(left) Some **ráths,** *or fairy forts, look like piles of stones. Others have been covered by moss and soil, and look like mounds of earth.*

(below) Celtic crosses still stand in many parts of the Irish countryside. The Celts carved images on the crosses as a way to tell Bible stories. The Cross of the Scriptures features carvings of Vikings who are believed to represent evil characters from the Bible.

Fairy forts

Many Irish believe that the Druids' magical powers can still be found in *ráths*, or fairy forts, throughout Ireland's countryside. *Ráths* are ruins of ancient houses in which the Celts lived. People fear that harm will come to them if they disturb the *ráths*. Some people are also careful not to destroy fairy thorns, or blackthorn trees. They believe that fairies meet in these bushes, which have tangled branches and thorns. Anyone who cuts down a fairy thorn will be cursed with bad luck.

Roman Catholicism

The Celts started trading goods with England at the end of 200 A.D. The English introduced the Celts to Roman Catholicism, which was the main religion in England and Europe at the time. Roman Catholicism is a **denomination** of Christianity. Christians believe in one God, and they worship Jesus Christ, who they believe is God's son on earth. After learning about Roman Catholicism, the Celts began to add Christian beliefs and practices to Druidism.

Saint Patrick and Saint Brigid

Saint Patrick (389–461) is one of Ireland's two patron **saints**. A patron saint is a special guardian who is believed to protect people. Saint Patrick devoted almost 30 years of his life to teaching the people of Ireland about Roman Catholicism. Celtic people had trouble believing in one Christian God because they were used to worshiping many gods and goddesses. Saint Patrick used the shamrock, a three-leaf **clover** that grew all over Ireland, to explain that God was made up of three parts: the father, the son, and the holy spirit. This symbol helped people who believed in many gods understand the Christian idea of one God.

Ireland's second patron saint is Saint Brigid. Saint Brigid was a nun, or a woman who devotes her life to God in the Roman Catholic faith, who founded one of the first Irish convents, called *Cill-Dara*. A convent is a place where nuns live, study, and pray.

The arrival of Protestantism

By the 1500s, some people in Europe began to question the power of the pope, who was the leader of the Roman Catholic Church. King Henry VIII, who ruled England and Ireland, was unhappy with many of the Church's rules. He changed England's religion from Roman Catholicism to Protestantism, another denomination of Christianity, and established the Church of England. The Church of England kept several beliefs and ceremonies of the Roman Catholic Church, but King Henry VIII made himself the religious leader.

Saint Patrick stands at the bottom of Croagh Patrick, a mountain named in his honor, in this illustration from the 1800s. The Irish believe there are no snakes in Ireland because Saint Patrick climbed the mountain, rang large silver bells, and scared all the snakes off the island.

Church of Ireland

King Henry VIII also made Protestantism Ireland's religion. Many Irish did not want to convert, or change their religion, and secretly kept their Roman Catholic beliefs. As punishment for disobeying Henry VIII, Irish Catholics lost many of their rights, including the right to own land.

Henry VIII established the Church of Ireland, another Protestant church, to control people who were not converting. His actions caused many years of fighting between Roman Catholics and Protestants in Ireland.

Christ Church Cathedral, built between 1172 and 1220, is the oldest cathedral in Ireland.

Pilgrimages

Many Irish Roman Catholics take trips to places in their country with religious importance. These journeys are called pilgrimages. Holy Island, in the west of Ireland, is a popular pilgrimage site. There, people visit ancient churches and ask God to forgive them for their sins. People also visit Holy Island's sacred well, which is believed to answer their prayers.

Many pilgrims visit Knock, in Northern Ireland, where a famous miracle is believed to have taken place in 1879. One evening, as two women passed the Knock Parish Church, three figures appeared before them. The images were of Jesus' mother, Mary; her husband, Joseph; and John the Baptist, a Christian saint. After the women saw the visions, other people saw them as well. The Roman Catholic Church called these visions a miracle. Today, more than one million pilgrims visit the church in Knock each year. Those who are sick believe they will be healed if they visit the site where the visions appeared.

The Knock Parish Church has an enormous courtyard that can hold up to 12,000 pilgrims at a time.

Christmas carolers entertain shoppers in downtown Dublin with traditional Irish Christmas carols such as "Come Home to Ireland for Christmas."

Irish holidays celebrate religion, music, history, harvests, sporting events, and the people of Ireland. One of the most important holidays is Christmas, on December 25, which celebrates the birth of Jesus Christ. In the weeks before Christmas, the streets of Irish towns and cities fill with Christmas markets where people buy gifts, decorations, and food. This tradition began with "Fair Day," when people gathered before Christmas to sell turkeys, geese, butter, eggs, and vegetables for holiday dinners.

Advent

The four weeks before Christmas are called Advent. When Advent begins, Irish priests and ministers place four candles on the altars of their churches. They light one candle each Sunday of Advent, until all candles are lit at the end of the four weeks.

Christmas Eve

On Christmas Eve, December 24, families often enjoy a special meal called a crimbo. The crimbo consists of stuffed turkey, ham covered in honey and cloves, potatoes, carrots, Brussels sprouts, gravy, and cranberry sauce. After dinner, families watch Christmas movies, play board games, sing Christmas carols, and tell stories. The eldest person tells the story of Mary and Joseph and the night that Jesus was born. Stories of Ireland's history and heroes are also part of the celebrations.

"First Light"

At midnight, many families go to a special church service, or mass. The service used to be called "First Light" because people were still at church when the sun came up. Before leaving for midnight mass, families light a red candle and place it in a front window of their home. The candle is a reminder of the trouble Mary and Joseph had finding a place to stay on the night that Jesus was born. People light candles to show Mary and Joseph the way.

Christmas Day

On Christmas Day, calls of *"Nollaig Shona Duit,"* which is Gaelic for "Merry Christmas," can be heard in many parts of Ireland. Families spend the day opening gifts, playing games, singing carols, and eating an elaborate dinner. The main part of the meal is usually a roast goose or turkey stuffed with potatoes and served with a large slice of ham under it. Another traditional Christmas dish is spiced beef. Twice a day, a week before it is cooked, people take their beef out of the refrigerator and rub spices, such as cloves, garlic, and pepper, on the meat to make it more flavorful.

After dinner, sweet desserts, such as Christmas cake and pudding, are served. Christmas cake is made from caramel mixed with dried fruits, almonds, flour, eggs, sugar, butter, and an alcoholic beverage called rum. Some people bake their Christmas cake in October — three months before Christmas! Baking the cake early allows all the flavors to blend together. The rum keeps the cake from becoming stale.

Two girls try to reach the door knocker on their friend's house, which is decorated with a wreath made from pine branches. In Ireland, people do not remove their Christmas decorations until January 6, which is called "Little Christmas," because they are afraid that they will have bad luck if they do.

During Christmas, many people put Nativity scenes, which show Jesus' birth, on their front lawns.

Lent

The most sacred holiday in Ireland is Easter. It marks the death of Jesus Christ and his return to life. The six weeks before Easter are called Lent. During Lent, people pray and ask forgiveness for their sins. They also fast, or give up their favorite food or drink. This **sacrifice** reminds them of the 40 days and nights that Jesus spent in the desert without food or water. Not eating or drinking was Jesus' way of asking God to forgive him for his sins.

Shrove Tuesday

The Tuesday before Lent begins is called Shrove Tuesday. It marks the last feast before Lent. In the past, people gave up foods such as milk, eggs, flour, and lard for Lent. They would make pancakes before the holiday to use up these ingredients. The tradition of eating pancakes on Shrove Tuesday continues today.

How many of these pancakes, prepared for Shrove Tuesday, can you eat?

On Good Friday, a Roman Catholic priest leads a religious procession, or orderly group, through the streets of Killarney, a city in the southwest of the Republic of Ireland.

Easter

The week before Easter is called Holy Week. Holy Week begins with Palm Sunday, which honors the day that Jesus returned from the desert. People go to church and watch processions, or solemn parades, where people carry statues of Jesus through the streets.

Five days later, people celebrate Good Friday, the day that Jesus was **crucified**. At a special mass on Easter Sunday, they remember Jesus Christ's Resurrection, or return to life. Families go to church in the morning. In the afternoon, children decorate Easter eggs with bright watercolor paints and help their families prepare the Easter Sunday dinner. This first large meal after Lent usually includes a roast lamb, potatoes, and other vegetables.

Saint Patrick's Day

Saint Patrick's Day, on March 17, honors Saint Patrick. It is one of the largest celebrations in the Republic of Ireland and Northern Ireland, as well as in many countries around the world. On Saint Patrick's Day, people watch parades in which bands and brightly colored floats travel down the main street. Many people dress in green, the color of Ireland's rolling countryside and one of Ireland's national colors. Green is also the color of shamrocks, a symbol of the Republic of Ireland. Some people believe that if you do not wear green on Saint Patrick's Day, you will have bad luck.

After the parades, people go to parties or to the local pub to meet friends. Some people treat Saint Patrick's Day as a religious holiday instead, and go to church to learn about Saint Patrick's life. After church, they have a small family celebration at home.

Saint Brigid's Day

February 1, is Saint Brigid's Day. Some Irish people remember this patron saint by going to a special church service. At school, children make a Saint Brigid's cross using sticks and wool. Traditionally, people put the cross under the **rafters** of their home to bring their families good luck, health, and fortune.

The sounds of bagpipes, drums, and xylophones can be heard during Saint Patrick's Day parades throughout Northern Ireland and the Republic of Ireland.

Samharin

Many people believe that the custom of dressing up in scary costumes and carving pumpkins on Halloween, as well as welcoming good spirits on All Souls' Day, on November 2, began with *Samharin*. *Samharin* means "the end of the warm season" in Gaelic. This ancient Celtic harvest festival is celebrated on October 31 or November 1. People who practiced Druidism believed that the spirits of the dead returned to earth for one night on *Samharin*. Some spirits were kind, and were welcomed by the people. Evil spirits needed to be scared away. To scare the evil spirits, people painted their faces, dressed up in costumes, and made jack-o'-lanterns out of turnips. Today, people continue these traditions on Halloween and on All Souls' Day, when they remember family members who are deceased by setting a place for them at the dinner table.

Children dressed in costumes go trick-or-treating on Halloween.

(above) Puck Fair is a popular harvest festival which is celebrated every August in Killorglin, a town in the southwest Republic. A goat called "the king of the fair" is paraded through the streets. The fair lasts for three days, called Gathering Day, Middle Day, and Scattering Day.

A matchmaking festival

Hundreds of years ago, in the small town of Lisdoonvarna, in western Ireland, people celebrated the end of the harvest season with the Lisdoonvarna Matchmaking Festival. Men and women were introduced to each other, in the hope that a match would be made and they would get married. This festival is still celebrated today, although people no longer try to make matches. The festival begins in September, after the harvest, with a brilliant fireworks display. It ends in the first week of October with a talent competition to choose the king and queen of the festival.

Music and dance

The people of Ireland have a long tradition of dancing, singing, and playing music. In ancient times, traveling bards, or singers, sang about events from other parts of Ireland. Eventually, these songs developed into songs about Irish heroes, true love, and **patriotism**. Today, performers, such as the popular folk singer Christy Moore, sing many of these traditional Irish songs.

Sean nós

Sean nós is a type of traditional Irish song sung by one person. The songs, which are written in Gaelic, are often unhappy songs about real people or events. Many tell of people who drowned at sea. *Sean nós* singers do interesting things with their voices, such as closing their throat in the middle of a note to stop the sound suddenly or holding a note for a very long time.

Irish instruments

Many traditional Irish songs were played on instruments such as the flute; the fiddle; the *bodhrán,* a hand-held drum; the accordion; the *fead*, or tin-whistle; and the Celtic harp. The Celtic harp is Ireland's national emblem, and it appears on all Irish coins. It is smaller than other harps and plays fewer notes because it does not have as many strings or any pedals.

Uillean pipes are another traditional instrument. They look like bagpipes, with many pipes coming out of a large sack and bellows that blow air into the sack. When the musician squeezes air out of the sack, the pipes play one long note. Shorter notes are played by covering certain holes on the pipes.

(above) A craftsperson makes a **bodhrán** *at his workshop by stretching goat skin over a beech wood frame.*

The fiddle, which looks like a small violin, is used to play many upbeat Irish songs. Musicians can play different notes very quickly as they move their bow back and forth between the strings.

Popular music

Many Irish folk and rock groups are popular around the world. Some groups, such as the Chieftains, play traditional Irish songs and sing in Gaelic. The Corrs, an Irish family, perform traditional and modern pop songs, and use Irish instruments, such as the fiddle, the *bodhrán*, and the *fead*. The Irish rock group U2 and singer-songwriter Sinead O'Connor sing about history and social problems in Ireland, such as the fighting in Northern Ireland. Enya, a singer and songwriter, combines traditional Celtic sounds with modern, electronic tones.

(right) Rock band U2 ends a tour at home in Dublin in front of Slane Castle.

[inset]: Two members of U2, the Edge and Bono, perform for Irish fans.

Traditional dance

Many traditional Irish dances have Celtic origins, including the popular step dance. Step dancers hold their arms at their sides, keep their upper bodies stiff, and perform complicated steps, often very quickly. They must have excellent balance in order to move their feet so quickly without using their arms to keep them steady. Speed and the number of steps a dancer has to do vary with each type of step dance.

Step dancers perform at special competitions called *feis* and at *ceilidhes,* which are gatherings that combine traditional music, dancing, and storytelling. Step dancing has also become popular in other countries, with groups such as *Riverdance* performing internationally. During the shows, the dancers, wearing elaborate, brightly colored costumes, perform fast, lively dances, which give a modern feeling to older traditional steps.

Step dancers wear very elaborate costumes during competitions.

Some of the oldest artifacts found in Ireland depict Celtic gods and goddesses such as this carving on a brass caldron, or cooking pot, from around 100 A.D.

Irish art has had many influences — beginning with Celtic styles of art, which date back to 300 B.C. Celtic art is characterized by symbols and shapes such as spirals, zigzags, and crosses. These symbols decorate bronze spears, books, jewelry, and other objects. Ireland's countryside and history are popular themes for more recent artists.

The Turoe Stone is one of the earliest examples of Celtic art found on the island. This large granite boulder, with spirals and curves carved into it, dates back to 100 or 200 B.C.

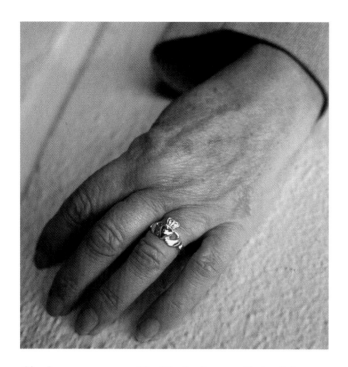

Claddagh rings

One of the best known examples of Celtic art is the Claddagh ring. Traditionally, on the day a woman in Ireland got married, she received a Claddagh ring from her mother. Three symbols appear on a Claddagh ring: a heart, for love; a crown, for loyalty; and two hands, for friendship.

The art of Aran

Craftspeople on the Aran Islands, off Ireland's west coast, are known for knitting sweaters with elaborate patterns. These sweaters were originally worn by fishers. Different patterns distinguished one family from another, so if someone drowned, he or she could be easily identified. Some patterns, which are still used today, were religious symbols or from nature. The moss stitch is a series of small, raised bumps that symbolizes the **fertility** of mossy soil. The honeycomb stitch, which looks like diamonds, symbolizes the rewards of hard work. The plaited, or braided, stitch is a complicated, tightly woven stitch that represents the closeness of families.

Single women wear Claddagh rings on their right hand, with the heart facing away from them. When they find friendship or love, they turn the ring to face them. When they are sure that they have found true love, they wear the ring on their left hand, with the heart toward them.

What patterns do you see on these Aran sweaters?

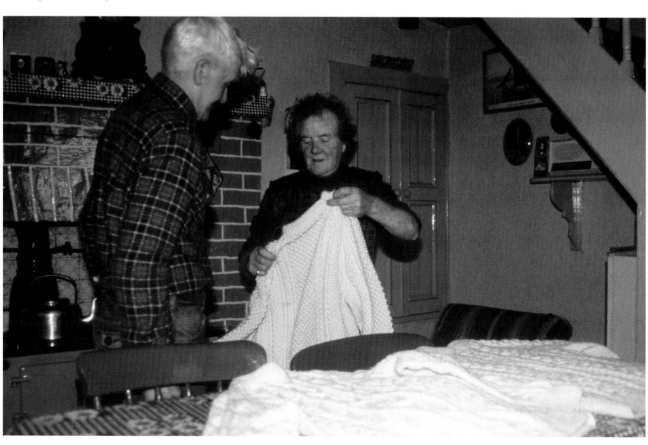

Patriotism in art

Many of Ireland's artists in the late 1800s and early 1900s were known for their patriotism. Before the Republic of Ireland gained independence from Britain in 1922, artists such as John Keating (1889–1977), Estella Solomons (1882–1968), and Maurice MacGonigal (1900–1979) promoted pride in their country through their paintings of historical events, Irish heroes, and Ireland's landscape.

Irish artists

Some Irish artists introduced European art styles to Ireland. Mainie Jellett (1879–1944) painted in a European style called cubism. In cubism, artists represent objects using geometric shapes and patterns. Jack Butler Yeats (1871–1957) is one of the best-known Irish painters of all time. Instead of painting people and landscapes as they really looked, he used blurry shapes and lines to portray them.

(above) The painting **Ruth with Teddy** *by Estella Solomons is of a girl from Dublin.*

(below) **The Death of Diarmud, The Last Handful of Water,** *by Jack Butler Yeats, portrays characters from Celtic mythology.*

(above) When archaeologists uncovered the Poulnabrone dolmen, in western Ireland, they found the remains of more than 25 people who had been buried thousands of years ago.

Hundreds of ancient ruins are scattered throughout Ireland's countryside. They range from **prehistoric** tombs to **monasteries** built mostly between 500 and 1100.

Portal tombs

Portal tombs, or dolmens, are large stone structures that **archaeologists** believe were built by **Neolithic** peoples. Neolithic peoples arrived in Ireland from Europe and the United Kingdom around 3500 B.C. The tombs were likely used to bury important people, such as tribal leaders, and for religious ceremonies. Each portal tomb is made of large slabs of stone standing upright, with another large slab resting on top of them to create an alcove, or small, sheltered area. Portal tombs were built to face east, so worshipers could see the rising sun.

(below) About 200,000 tons (181,500 metric tons) of stone were used to build the Newgrange passage tomb, which measures 200 feet (68 meters) across and 20 feet (6 meters) high.

Passage tombs

Prehistoric peoples also built passage tombs to bury their religious and tribal leaders. A passage tomb is a large, circular structure with a burial chamber inside. The chamber can be reached by following underground tunnels. Newgrange, in eastern Ireland, is the most famous passage tomb in the country. Its construction began around 3200 B.C. and lasted more than 70 years.

Archaeologists excavating, or digging up, the Newgrange tomb between 1962 and 1975 made a startling discovery. Each year on December 21, the first day of winter, the sun shines through the tomb's main entrance, down the 62-foot (19-meter) long main passage, and lights up the burial chamber at the tomb's center. This discovery suggests that ancient peoples were studying the sun, making Newgrange the oldest known solar **observatory** in the world.

The Skellig Michael monastery is made up of six buildings and two small chapels used for religious ceremonies and prayer. Each beehive-shaped building was made by overlapping flat stones, so no cement was needed to hold them together.

Monasteries

Monasteries and the ruins of monasteries can be found throughout Ireland. A monastery is where Christian holy men, called monks, live, work, and practice their religion. The monastery provides the monks with silence and solitude, which they believe are important to their studies and worship. In Ireland, monks **transcribed** books, such as the Bible, and taught people about Christianity. Over time, Irish monasteries became religious, political, and artistic centers. One of the few monasteries that is still standing is Skellig Michael, located on the Iveragh Peninsula, in southwestern Ireland. Skellig Michael sits on a ledge 700 feet (213 meters) above the sea. To reach it, people must climb 600 stone steps!

The castles of Ireland

The Rock of Cashel stands on a hill in southern Ireland. The Rock was not only used as a castle and a monastery, but also as a fortress, where kings and wealthy families were protected from attackers.

Beginning in the 1100s, Ireland's kings and wealthy families lived in castles where they and their property were protected from invaders. Blarney Castle, near the city of Cork, is one of the most famous castles in the world. Blarney Castle was built in 1446 by Dermot MacCarthy, who was one of the rulers of Ireland at the time. The main part of the castle, called the "stone," is a large, square building with several narrow windows. A parapet, or low wall that helps defend the castle, surrounds the top of the "stone."

A magical stone

When Dermot MacCarthy built the castle, he put a very special stone, now called the Blarney stone, into the parapet wall. People believe that anyone who kisses the stone will be given the gift of **eloquent** speech.

Many stories explain the Blarney stone. One tells of Cormac Teige MacCarthy, the Lord of Blarney, who was one of the last descendants of Dermot MacCarthy to live in Blarney Castle. While he was living there, the English, under Queen Elizabeth I, took over many parts of Ireland, including the land that Blarney Castle was on. She demanded that the Irish living on her land follow her rules. Lord Blarney kept failing to obey her rules. Instead, he gave the queen many long-winded stories. The queen said he was full of "blarney," which described a person who speaks in a smooth and flattering way when trying to trick someone.

People from all over the world visit Blarney Castle. Kissing the Blarney stone is not easy! People must lie on their backs with their head tilted upside down as they hold iron bars for support.

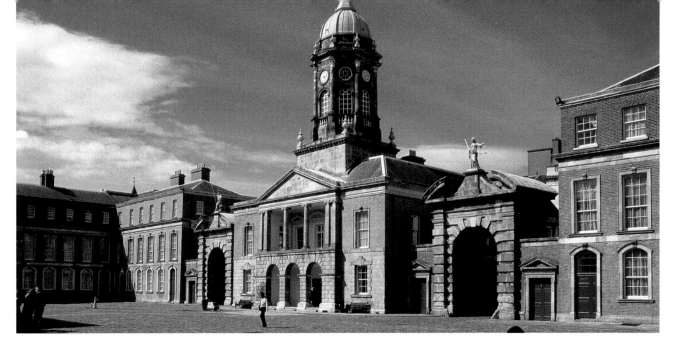

Dublin castle was once a fortress built by Anglo Norman settlers in the 1200s. Today, parts of the castle are used as government offices.

Dublin Castle

Dublin Castle was built in 1204 for King John of England, who ruled Ireland at the time. The castle is made up of many separate buildings and towers, which are linked together to form a courtyard. One of the most famous parts of Dublin Castle is the throne room, which is decorated with crystal chandeliers and paintings of Greek gods and goddesses. Today, Irish presidents are inaugurated, or sworn in, in Saint Patrick's Hall, one of Dublin Castle's main rooms.

Dunluce Castle

To reach the ruins of Dunluce Castle, on the north coast of Northern Ireland, people must cross a very narrow bridge. The ruins stand on a piece of land that is separated from the mainland by a deep gorge, or gap. Construction on the castle began in the 1300s. Over the next 300 years, it was home to two of Ireland's most powerful families, the MacDonnells and the MacQuillans. People lived in the castle until 1636, when part of the cliff that it stood on fell into the sea, taking the kitchen and some servants along with it.

The ruins of Dunluce Castle stand nearly 100 feet (30 meters) above the North Channel, on the rocky coast of Northern Ireland.

Speaking English and Gaelic

The official language of both Northern Ireland and the Republic of Ireland is English. The Republic of Ireland has a second official language called Gaelic, also known as Irish. People in different parts of the Republic speak different dialects, or versions, of Gaelic.

Changing Gaelic

Gaelic is an ancient Celtic language. At first, it was written using a very basic method, called Ogham writing, in which a group of lines represented each sound. One sentence might be made up of hundreds of lines!

Gaelic began to change when Christian **missionaries** came to Ireland in 400 A.D. Many missionaries knew how to read and write **Latin**, which was much simpler than Ogham writing. They used Latin symbols, or letters, to represent the Gaelic sounds. This created a problem because the Latin alphabet had only eighteen symbols and letters, while the Gaelic language had more than 60 sounds. As a result, many Gaelic words changed or were lost.

(top) Students from a school in Galway, on the west coast, do a presentation in Gaelic. Some Gaelic words they have learned are posted around the classroom.

The arrival of the English

Over the next thousand years, other groups that invaded Ireland influenced the Gaelic language. When the Normans invaded England and Ireland in the 1100s, they brought French and English with them. During English rule, there were times when the Irish were not allowed to speak or write Gaelic, although some people used the language in secret.

Gaelic today

By the 1900s, Gaelic had almost disappeared from Ireland. Since then, the Irish have tried to revive their language. In 1922, when the Republic of Ireland declared its independence from Britain, it made Gaelic an official language. Today, students in the Republic learn Gaelic in school, although they speak English in everyday conversation. In a few parts of Ireland, some people speak only Gaelic. Many of these areas, known as the *Gaeltachts*, are in Galway and the Aran Islands, in western Ireland. People who live in these areas have been able to preserve their language and traditions because they have little contact with the rest of the country.

(top, right) These friends from Northern Ireland speak English to one another.

(below) Street signs in parts of the Republic are written in English and Gaelic.

English	Gaelic
Hello.	*Dia dhuit.* (pronounced DEE-ah ghith)
See you later.	*Slán go fóill.* (pronounced SLAWN guh foal)
Good morning.	*Maidin mhaith.* (pronounced MAH-jun vah)
Good night.	*Oiche mhaith.* (pronounced EEH-ha vah agut)
Please.	*Le do thoil.* (pronounced leh duh HILL)
Thank you.	*Go raibh maith agat.* (pronounced guh rev mah ah-guth)
You're welcome.	*Tá fáilte romhat.* (pronounced TAH FALL-cheh ROW-at)

Storytelling has been an important part of Irish culture for thousands of years. Druids memorized and told more than 350 stories about Irish kings, gods, goddesses, giants, and warriors. Eventually, each town or village in Ireland had a storyteller who told tales about gods, goddesses, and Celtic heroes fighting in great battles.

Cuchulain

Cuchulain is the most famous Celtic warrior in Irish mythology. He was an enormous, strong man with seven fingers on each hand and seven toes on each foot. Cuchulain was very smart and could perform magic, such as changing into a creature that was half-man, half-beast during battles. In Cuchulain's most famous battle, he defended what is now Northern Ireland from enemy forces all by himself.

A Druid storyteller tells a story and plays the harp for a group of Celtic warriors.

Fionn MacCumhaill

Fionn MacCumhaill was another mythical Irish warrior. He led the Fianna, a group of soldiers and knights who protected the high king, or Celtic ruler, of Ireland. According to one legend, MacCumhaill burned his thumb in a fire and had to suck it to stop the bleeding. The blood gave him the ability to see the future. Many people believe that this power allowed him to protect Ireland.

Fairies

Traditionally, some Irish believed in fairies. These tiny, imaginary creatures were thought to have magical powers, such as the ability to change people or objects from one thing to another. People were afraid of fairies because they believed that fairies had the power to harm them and bring bad luck. In Donegal, a town in the northwest part of the Republic, many gateposts have sharp ends so fairies would hurt themselves if they rested there.

Fairies and tiny animals such as birds, snails, and butterflies parade through a field in Ireland, in this illustration from the 1800s.

Irish literature

During some periods of English rule in Ireland, people were not allowed to celebrate their Irish traditions or to read books by Irish authors. Beginning in the 1600s, some Irish writers began to criticize the way the English treated the Irish. Jonathan Swift (1667–1745) was an Irish novelist and poet who lived in England. Swift used humor to criticize the hardships that the English caused the Irish. His most famous novel, *Gulliver's Travels*, was about a man lost at sea who met people from strange and different places. In the book, Swift used make-believe people and places to criticize the society in which he lived.

*After Gulliver, the main character in **Gulliver's Travels**, is shipwrecked, he swims to Liliput, an imaginary land where the people, called Liliputians, are 6 inches (15 centimeters) tall. In this illustration, Gulliver is attacked by the Liliputians with tiny arrows as he tries to walk to shore.*

The Book of Kells

The Book of Kells is a Celtic **manuscript** that dates back to the 800s. It is a Latin translation of four sections of the New Testament, part of the Bible. The Book of Kells was transcribed by monks and is an illuminated manuscript, which means that paintings and patterns decorate the pages. Among the illustrations are plants and animals, such as snakes and birds, which are important symbols in the Bible. The pages were made from calfskin, and all the words and drawings were carefully done by hand. To keep this delicate book from being damaged, it is kept in a glass case at the Trinity College Library in Dublin. Every day, a page is turned, so visitors see something new each time they visit.

An illustration from the Book of Kells shows Saint Matthew, who is believed to have written the first section of the New Testament that is in the Book of Kells.

James Joyce not only wrote novels, he also wrote three books of poetry, and a well-known collection of stories called **The Dubliners.**

The Irish Literary Revival

During the 1800s and early 1900s, a new group of writers formed a **movement** known as the Irish Literary Revival. This group, which included James Joyce, William Butler Yeats, and George Russell, wrote about their love for Ireland and their belief that Ireland should be independent from Britain.

James Joyce

James Joyce (1882–1941) moved from Ireland to Europe, but Dublin and the surrounding Irish countryside remained the focus of his works. His most famous book, *Ulysses*, follows the main character, a man named Leopold Bloom, as he walks through Dublin on one day, June 16. Each year, on June 16, which is called Bloomsday, people from all over the world come to Dublin to look at the same sites, walk along the same streets, and even stop for a drink at the same pub that Leopold visited in Joyce's book.

Modern literature

Today, Irish writers and poets continue to entertain and educate their readers with both humorous and serious stories about life in Ireland. Maeve Binchy (1940–) writes about Irish society in her newspaper articles, novels, and plays. Roddy Doyle (1958–) is a novelist whose works focus on Ireland's history and everyday life. In 1997, Doyle won the Booker Prize, an international award for outstanding literature, for his novel *Paddy Clarke Ha Ha Ha*. He wrote this novel from the perspective of a ten-year-old boy growing up in Dublin. Seamus Heaney is an Irish poet who won a **Nobel Prize** for literature in 1995. Many of Heaney's poems are about the hardships that the Irish people have faced.

Modern theater

Theater is another important way in which the Irish tell stories. George Bernard Shaw (1856–1950) and Samuel Beckett (1906–1989) are among the best-known Irish playwrights. Shaw won the Nobel Prize for literature in 1925, and Beckett won the same prize in 1969.

During his career, George Bernard Shaw wrote more than 50 plays, using humor to describe Irish society, politics, and people's beliefs. In *Pygmalion*, he tells about a character named Henry Higgins, who tutors an unschooled woman named Eliza Doolittle. This play, which criticizes English society, later became a musical called *My Fair Lady*. Samuel Beckett is best known for his play *Waiting for Godot*, in which two characters wait for Godot, a character who never appears.

Many of Ireland's playwrights, including William Butler Yeats and John Synge, have focused on the themes of Irish history, patriotism, and rural life. More recent dramatists have concentrated on modern issues facing Irish society. The plays of Tom Murphy (1935–) describe **emigration** from Ireland and recent changes to Irish society. Popular playwright Anne Devlin has made the tensions in Northern Ireland the theme of her plays.

Irish plays are performed in theaters throughout the world. Actors Carli Norris and Roy Marsden play Eliza Doolittle and Henry Higgins in a production of **Pygmalion** *in London, England.*

An Irish tale

According to Irish folklore, leprechauns live all through the Irish countryside. These elves are often portrayed as small, grumpy shoemakers who hide pots full of gold. Legend has it that you can find a leprechaun by following the sound of the shoemaker's hammer. If you catch a leprechaun and manage to hold on to him, he has to give you his pot of gold. If you take your eyes off him, though, he will disappear and take his gold with him!

Patrick and the leprechaun

One fine evening, as Patrick O'Donnell was walking home from the Donegal county fair, he heard a shrill cry coming from the **bog**. "'Tis not the sound of a baby's cry, and 'tis not the sound of an animal stuck in the bush, so I'd better go have a look," he said.

After passing one thorn bush after another, he came to the bush where the crying was coming from. A tiny, little man was caught on a thorn by his tiny suspenders! Beneath the bush was a tiny cobbler's bench covered in tiny bits of leather and nails.

"Aha!" Patrick exclaimed, "You must be a leprechaun!" The leprechaun stopped crying. "If I am or if I am not, 'tis a small matter to you. Take me off this bush or I will die. And be careful with my suspenders, for they are brand new."

Patrick O'Donnell carefully unhooked the little man from the thorn, but would not let him go. "'Tis a leprechaun you are, and I'll keep my eyes on you until you tell me where your pot of gold is hidden."

The leprechaun angrily took Patrick to another part of the bog, far away. "'Tis under that bush there," the leprechaun said grumpily.

"You're sure?" Patrick O'Donnell asked.

The leprechaun replied, "As sure as I'm the tiny man who mends the shoes of all the fairies after their long nights of dancing."

Excitedly, Patrick rushed toward the thorn bush. "But I've no spade to dig with, and if I go home to get one, how will I remember which bush to look under when I get back?"

"Well now," the leprechaun replied. "'Tis your problem, not my own."

Suddenly, Patrick thought of a solution. "I know! If I tie my handkerchief around one of the bush's branches, I'll remember where you've hidden the pot of gold."

Patrick, sure that he had found his fortune, let the leprechaun go. In an instant, the leprechaun disappeared.

It took Patrick the rest of the night to get home and back again. As the sun was rising, Patrick tramped through the bog, excited about digging up his gold.

He walked and walked, until he was halfway through the thorn bushes. Suddenly, he stopped, astonished by what he saw. Tied around every single thorn bush in the middle of the bog was a handkerchief, exactly the same as the one Patrick tied to the thorn bush the leprechaun had shown him!

The leprechaun had tricked him, and Patrick O'Donnell lost his pot of gold forever.

Glossary

archaeologist A person who studies the past by looking at buildings and artifacts

bog An area of soft, wet land

clover A plant with leaves of three leaflets and small, rounded flowers

crucify To put to death by nailing to a cross

custom Something that a group of people has done for so long that it becomes an important part of their way of life

denomination An organized religious group within a faith

eloquent Expressive and effective speech

emigration Leaving one country for another

fertility Being able to produce abundant crops or vegetation

independent Not governed by a foreign power

Latin The language of the ancient Romans

manuscript A document written by hand, before the invention of printing

missionary A person who travels to a foreign country to spread a particular religion

monastery A building where monks live and work according to religious rules

movement The activities of a group of people who are trying to achieve a goal

myth A traditional story that explains mysterious events or ideas and is usually about a god or another being with superhuman powers

Neolithic Belonging to the period after the Mesolithic age, when prehumans used stone tools, farmed, and began pottery and weaving

Nobel Prize A prize granted annually to people who made outstanding contributions in areas such as literature, medicine, and the promotion of peace

observatory A place where the stars and planets are studied

patriotism Love of and loyalty to one's country

prehistoric Belonging to the time before recorded history

rafter A beam that supports a roof

sacrifice The act of giving up something that is important or valued for the sake of something or someone else

saint A person recognized by a religious faith as being holy

transcribe To copy in writing

United Kingdom A group of countries that includes England, Scotland, Wales, and Northern Ireland

worship To honor or respect a god

Index

1 2 3 4 5 6 7 8 9 0 Printed in the USA 5 4 3 2

Ireland breeds world-famous racehorses

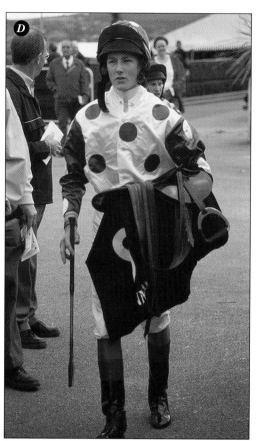

A. Horseracing fans watch from the grandstand.

B. Betting on the races is done through a person called a bookie or bookmaker.

C. The winning horse and jockey get their picture taken in the winner's circle.

D. A jockey's racing clothes are called silks. The design of the shirt identifies the horse's owner.

E. The area just before the finish line is called the homestretch.

Dublin's St. Saviours Amateur Boxing Club

A. Boxers from the St. Saviours Amateur Boxing Club in Dublin.

B. The main object of boxing is to learn to defend yourself, not to hurt your opponent.

C. A young boxer gets tips from the club's coach, John McCormack. As a young man, John was an Irish boxing champion.

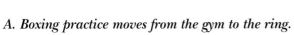

A. Boxing practice moves from the gym to the ring.

B. Upper body strength is especially important for boxing.

C. Skipping rope gives boxers fast feet in the ring.

D. These boxers are learning to protect themselves from each other's punches.

E. A young boxer practices his punches against a punching bag.